More from avid

Poems for People Who Don't Read Poetry

Before I read Genevieve's work, I would never consider reading a book of poetry—poems often mystify me.

—Kathy Belicki, Professor Emeritus of Psychology

I didn't appreciate how much poetry and music have in common until I was introduced to Genevieve's poems and prose. The more I read, the more engaged I became.

—Anne Aspler, Emergency Physician, Professor, Singer

Genevieve's visually vivid poetry engages me the way films do. Her work is witty, evocative, and emotionally raw.

—Yuanda Zheng, Literacy & Numeracy Educator

I haven't read poetry since university and enjoyed finding the muscles again. An accessible body of work.

—Ian Taylor, Payments Executive

Poets can be like jazz musicians, enjoying themselves while leaving the audience behind, but Genevieve's approach is inclusive and very reader friendly.

—Maribeth Graham, Teacher

Genevieve forges perceptual tools for a disrupted world."

—Andrew Boyd, IT Consultant

[illegible] readers on *If I were God*:

[illegible]

If I Were God

If I Were God

Poems for People Who Don't Read Poetry

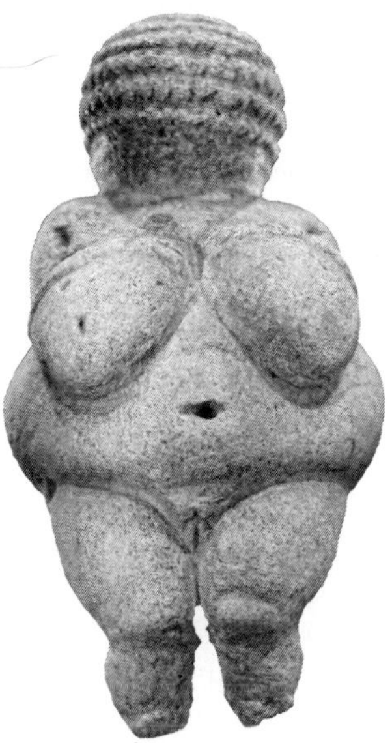

Genevieve Chornenki

Published by Brandon House Books
genevieve.chornenki@bell.net

ISBN: 978-1-7774963-0-2 (softcover)
ISBN: 978-1-7774963-1-9 (eBook)

Editor: Shaughnessy Bishop-Stall

Cover photo: *The Venus of Willendorf* (between 24,000 and
22,000 BCE). Naturhistorisches Museum, Vienna, Austria.
By Bjørn Christian Tørrissen, under multi-
license with GFDL and Creative Commons CC-BY 2.5

Cover and book design, layout and typesetting by
Jan Westendorp/katodesignandphoto.com

Printed and bound in Canada

To the memory of my brother Bob, who needed
no lessons on how to live in the present moment.

To David &
Mary

Best,

[illegible]

For most people, the matter isn't so much not liking poetry as feeling somehow overmatched, as if it were a contest and the other side had better equipment and more skill. Or as more than one student has said to me over the years, "I like poetry, but I don't understand it."

How To Read Poetry Like A Professor

—Thomas C. Foster

Contents

Part 3—If I Were God

Part 4—The Eternal Return

Introduction: Poems for People Who Don't Read Poetry—Lessons from Ottolenghi

Not only do I collect cookbooks, I *read* them, especially the personalized introductions that precede individual recipes. I lie on the couch or sprawl at the kitchen table, soaking up details. I'm as interested in how Sami Tamimi and Yotam Ottolenghi experienced *falafel* when they were boys in Jerusalem as I am in what Giuliano Bugialli says about pencil-thin asparagus for *Pasta con Asparagi.* I'm hungry for supplementary material about related people and places, traditions and techniques. So when I try out a recipe, I'm engaged on multiple levels.

I own almost as many poetry books as cookbooks—collections of selected poems, translations, anthologies—but few of them have the kind of introductions that engage me with the poets and their work. Verses might be placed in categories, and notes might appear at the end of a book, but there is rarely material about a poem's antecedents, especially from the poet. I want to know! What prompted the poem? Who or what influenced the poet? Why was one poetic form chosen over another? What tidbit of specialized knowledge would enhance my understanding—and I don't mean Norton footnotes that inform me that "Delhi" is a city in India.

Many who consider themselves to be practising poets insist that a poem "should stand on its own," even though they know that poetry is far less accessible to readers than cooking instructions. As one poet confessed, "Poets are like jazz musicians up on a stage. They're having a good time with each other, but what about the audience?" Well—why not change that by giving more attention to readers?

In the third edition of *Poetry: A Pocket Anthology*, editor R.S. Gwynn described the reaction that his first-year literature students had to a reading by a poet whom they had studied only in print:

> At the next class meeting . . . the comments that surface most often have to do with how much more meaningful the poems in the textbook become when the poet explains how he came to write them, how one poem is actually spoken in the voice of his dead father, how another is addressed to a friend who was paralyzed in an automobile accident. While these things could perhaps be inferred from the poems alone, the students are unanimous in their opinion that knowing the details beforehand adds a great deal to the impression the poem makes. As one student put it, "It's just that a poem makes a lot more sense when you know who's talking and when and where it's supposed to be taking place."
>
> "It always helps to know where poetry starts," adds another one of her classmates."

It has been years since I first read Professor Gwynn's words, but they stayed with me and guided me in creating these prose-verse combinations.

Poetry is an art form, a craft, a form of self-expression, a way of putting words to what can't be said. But, to me, it is above all a form of communication. Yes, I want my poems to be evocative, but I do not want to evoke confusion. If the poem is about displaced people, I don't want readers to think it's about the Virgin Mary. I ask, can readers understand what I am talking about without their having to exert too much effort *and* without my controlling their experience (a futile task, in any event) or pre-empting the poems? The prose that accompanies my poems is intended to enhance the reader's understanding and experience, to make the poems accessible.

Prose-poetry combinations are not, of course, my invention. I am merely riffing on an established literary genre, and there are other, more fulsome and famous prosimetra—*The Consolation of Philosophy* by Boethius (d. 524 CE) and *La Vita Nuova* by Dante Alighieri (d.1321 CE).

Twenty-first century writers have also made effective use of the prosimetrum. Kurdish refugee Behrouz Boochani won multiple awards for *No Friend But the Mountain,* a prose-verse autobiography that chronicles his incarceration in the Australian-run Manus Island detention centre. And accomplished British poet Ruth Padel published *We Are All From Somewhere Else: Migration and Survival in Poetry and Prose*. She had this to say about her composite form:

> . . . I wrote the poems, then added the prose to set them in context. The prose interludes are not essays but introductions to each of the poems—as in a live reading poets introduce poems with a little information, so the audience knows something about them when they listen.

Like Padel's prose, mine was added after I crafted a poem—to set it in context and in order to orient readers—without my being directive. Sometimes I use prose to explain what prompted a poem, such as an email from a stranger, or to acknowledge the influence and example of other poets like Auden and Bishop. Sometimes I use prose to convey obscure or esoteric facts, like what Hildegard of Bingen wrote in 1141 CE. And sometimes I use it to explain poetic jargon, as much to remind myself what it means as to edify the reader.

All of that said, I hope that the prose segments of this collection are enjoyable independent of the poems—just as Ottolenghi's prose entertains me without my having to chop onions and cilantro. But if readers prefer to taste the poem first, by all means!

Part 1

Moon Upon Moon

Encoded

When I was growing up, the household lexicon did not include
I love you.

Encoded

I want to show you something was all she had said
that late spring afternoon.
Dirt road and dust, old Chevrolet,
the warming breeze of lengthening days,
bobolink song that bubbled and sputtered,
one tumbled barn and shortly another.

She pulled off the road a few miles along,
the bumper grazing a clearing forlorn
and strewn with construction debris,
foundation bricks from another time
encircled by lanky, exhausted pines.
Unclaimed corn stover lay to the left,
newly built townhomes commanding the rest.
Here?

In answer she smiled to herself, face softening,
eyes fixed on something a little way off,
her nod the merest gesture of offering.
Then all at once, the boisterous shock of it
—wanton, imperial masses of Sweet Rocket!
Stalks as tall as any man
jostling skyward
lathered in lavender, lilac, mauve, cream, white.
Purple pandemonium:
every shade of pastel,
every note of perfumed opium.
Moths and bees swooning.
Bacchus crouching behind an old well.

On Pocketing a Flake of Sandstone from Clachtoll Broch

"Where is the bloody thing?"

"Dunno. Maybe we should follow that stone wall."

My partner, William, and I slip on wet machair and dodge sheep droppings, looking for the Clachtoll Broch, an Iron Age dwelling somewhere on the shore of the North Minch[1]. It is raining and visibility is poor, and we left our rain gear in the cabin at Inverkirkaig.

"Chuck it," I say. "Let's go find coffee."

Three days later, on our second attempt, we find the remains of a circular sandstone building a kilometre beyond where we'd turned back. It's on a ledge above the sea. The tide is out, and a viridian tide pool beguiles.

I enter the broch under a triangular-shaped lintel and immediately notice a greenblack stone with a deep bowl in its centre—a giant mortar without a pestle. Later I learn that archeologists had found partially processed barley grains in the bowl. The grains were charred, indicating that the broch met its end by fire.

On Pocketing a Flake of Sandstone from Clachtoll Broch

Thou shalt not covet thy neighbour's house
though it stand alone on a rocky knoll
and proclaim dominion over all.
Though its red stone walls be double-thick
and a massive boulder straddle its door.
Though age-worn quernstones line its floor
where barleycorns skirr in a knocking stone.
Neither shall thy covet thy neighbour's field
or anything within his realm.
Not his soapstone lamp nor his cheese nor his butter
from sheep that grow fat while they graze on the machair.
And the green tidal pool where he bathes—let it be
for shortly it will be claimed by the sea.
Gales will come and water roar,
crags and boulders set themselves square,
mice bury down in dry rushes and reeds
where his people sleep
while a spark from the hearth
catches the bracken thatch
and hungered flames leap.

Weapons of Past Destruction

"Can you direct me to the beheading machine?" I asked the docent at the entrance to the Scottish National Museum.

"The *be*—? Ah, yes," he said, "*The Maiden*. You'll find her in the Monarchy and Power display on Level 1."

Two-hundred years before the French Revolution, the Scots were decapitating people with an iron and oak contraption that could be taken apart and moved from place to place. Adulterers, forgers, murderers, robbers—at least 150 people, including two women, placed their necks on the crossbar as part of a public spectacle.

I found *The Maiden* where the docent said it would be, along with more, much more—axes, swords, shields, lances, pikes, daggers, and a cabinet of thumb screws known by a variety of pet names that include *Pilniewinks* and *Thumbkin*.

What kind of mind comes up with this stuff?

"Weapons of Past Destruction" is a pantoum, a wave-like poetic form that goes four steps forward and two back before circling round to the beginning. I chose this repetitive form because it so closely matches the subject matter.

Weapons of Past Destruction

—National Museum of Scotland, Level I,
Kingdom of the Scots: Monarchy and Power

Ingenuity—I mean the male mind—
finds infinite ways to kill and maim
displayed in technologies left behind.
No matter the cause, the outcome's the same.

See, infinite ways to kill and maim:
a spike downs the horse, double blade does the rest.
No matter the cause, the outcome's the same;
the one who dies quickly is the most blessed.

Spike downs the horse, double blade does the rest,
whinnies and shrieks, pleas for mercy or mother
—the one who dies quickly is the most blessed.
Such honour, such grace to dispatch one another.

Puddles of blood, pleas for mercy or mother,
a blade with a weight serves a higher purpose.
Such honour, such grace to dispatch one another
in the monarch's name, a most courtly service.

A blade with a weight serves a higher purpose;
it plummets right quick to sever the neck.
In the monarch's name, a courtly service
that moves a keen crowd to greater effect.

A blade plummets quickly, severs the neck
though sometimes the fingers avail as well
for they move a man to greatest effect
when death is replaced by limitless hell.

Yes, often the fingers avail as well:
two bars, one screw, tiny twists do the rest
where death is deferred by limitless hell.
She screams. No one hears. She is the least blessed.

Yet poetry sings in the names left behind:
The Maiden, the *Jedwart Stave*, *Pilniewinks*, too
So much ingenuity—ah, the male mind!
Give credit and praise where tribute is due.

Emergents

One particular Canadian publisher of poetry, a prominent one, invites submissions from "those debuting later in life," while other publishers speak of "emerging poets." All of which prompts a question: Is a euphemism a courtesy or a condescension?

Emergents

We sightless ones drawing root sap
thirteen years or more,
waxen and white in silent slots,
pinioned by demands of the day
—diapers and dubious careers
memos and deadlines—
now moult and creep to the light.

Not to mate and die—such waste!
but for our ravenous eyes
and the songs they stir.
Not for the praise of peers
or those curious ears
straining to gauge our heft
nor the worry of success,
the journal acceptance, the publisher's yes.

But for the rough touch of bark
the set of our wings
the scent of coming rain
a belly full of air.

Pass the Harp

Cædmon was an illiterate English cowherd. When the harp came his way during a feast, he headed for the door so he didn't have to improvise a song. But one night, a dream visitor insisted that he sing, and Cædmon spontaneously composed a hymn of praise about creation. Or so the story goes.

A rough, condensed translation of "Cædmon's Hymn" is "Let us praise the Lord for creating this wondrous world for humankind." But the text looks very strange to speakers of contemporary English like me:

Nu sculon herigean heofronice Weard
Meotodes meahte and his modgeþane
weorc Wuldor-Fæder swa he wundra gehwæs
ece Drihten or onstealde
He ærest sceop ealda bearnum
heofron to hrofe halig Scyppend
ða middengeard moncynnes Weard
ece Drihten æfter teode
firum foldan Frea ælmihtig,

When I read up on the piece, I learned that the lines of "Cædmon's Hymn" (like the lines of "Beowulf") are made up of two halves divided by a sharp pause. The halves are knit together by alliteration—***Meotodes*** ***m****eahte / and his* ***m****odgeþane*—and there are four beats to a line. But the words are incomprehensible to most of us, so we can't readily see that the names and attributes of *God* are stated and restated throughout the poem: WuldorFæder (*glory father*), Weard (*guardian*), Meotodes (*maker*), Drihten (*lord*), Scyppend *(creator*), and Frea (*master*).

I did not dare to reproduce all of the features of "Caedmon's Hymn" when writing "Pass the Harp." I used only alliteration. Even so, my challenge was not to sound like Gerard Manley Hopkins in "Binsey Poplars."

> My aspens dear, whose airy cages quelled,
> Quelled or quenched in leaves the leaping sun . . .

Pass the Harp

—to the memory of Cædmon

What reason the rippling rabbit
steps from the city sidewalk, so small,
with sun-shot ears and sand-coloured fur,
gumming the greenest grass, clover tips,
alert to the flutter of thistle down
as to the thrum of an engine?

What object the oak nursling
taken from the forest,
trapped in terra cotta,
unfurling one fragile frill
then another
while leaves at the crown crust and curl?

And what of the gleaming black ant
frantic on floor tiles and grout-valleys,
repeatedly resurrecting beneath my runners
until I bend down
and pinch hard
between sheets of paper towel?

The Orkney Hood

Jacqui Wood is not just an archeologist. She's an *experimental* archeologist—someone who studies how people did things in the past through trial and error—and she has a deep interest in "the practical aspects of daily life of prehistoric Europe." Wood has demonstrated prehistoric cooking techniques at the Biskupin Archaeological Festival in Poland, replicated the grass cape, shoes, and scabbard of Otzi the Iceman for the South Tyrol Museum of Archeology in Bolzano, Italy, and reconstructed an ancient furnace in a hillock in front of her house in Cornwall, England.

Wood contends that the skills needed to survive in the northern European landscape can be "very easily acquired" if "approached purely by logic."

In 2001, she was commissioned by the Tankerness Museum in Kirkwall, Orkney, to replicate a child's head-covering from the Iron Age (1200–600 BC) that had been found in a peat bank. The assignment took Wood five months of painstaking trial and error work. In the process, she concluded that four different people spun the yarn used in the main fabric and that the hood's extravagant fringe was recycled from a wealthy person's garment.

Was the Orkney hood accidentally lost in the bog or deliberately placed there as a votive offering?

The Orkney Hood

Raindrops and dew overfill a lochan
in the heather-silent bog,
a gloaming space,
a beckoning place
where a dun-coloured hood enters an opening out of time
—a child's cowl let fall by grieving hands.

Moon upon moon upon moon,
low clouds swaddle it,
moss and sedge shield it
from the curlew's spirit-wailing
and the charms of the night-scented orchid.
Moon upon moon

till men flaying a bank in fog-filled air
cleave its sepulchre—
—light and heat and incense of heather pour out!
wilder than a tempest, sharper than a dagger.
A hell-spirit not, but the cowl,
glowing, gilded, glorious.

Hand-shadows, too,
sleek with lanolin.
Fingers pluck fleece from moorit ewes
pull out bracken bits
drop spindle whorls
ply yarn
thread looms, throw shuttles,

weave two-by-two twill for the hood's pixie-pointed peak,
chevron bands for the shoulders, neck.
And the fringe—oh, the fringe!
pea tendrils long as a lamb shank:
fourteen-hundred fine woolen threads
twenty-one thousand twists
three-hundred-and-fifty catkins that once circled
        a chieftain's waist,
reworked for the curls of a peedie red-head.

Grandfather

Grandfather is a spectre. A will-o'-whisp. No, a piñata! He sways in and out of sight above my head, just beyond the reach of my stick. I want to give him a solid whack to spill his secrets, but he bares only bits of himself.

I've seen his photograph, his obituary, his grave in the Brookside Cemetery, his trace in census records. An unmarried male. A boarder at 514 Pritchard Avenue, Winnipeg. An Austrian immigrant digging city sewers. A plasterer, a boardman. Chornenki, Czornenky, Czornenki, Crnuk. Pavel, Paulus, Paul. He came to Canada in 1902—or was it 1903—when he was 18—or was that 19 or 20 years of age?

I can't assemble the man. The parts are inconclusive. I did not know him, and except for my father once saying he came from "Khorostiv," my parents never spoke of him. They were too busy raising four thoroughly anglicized children. But I have always wondered what prompted Grandfather to come to Canada, an initiative which gave his descendants access to advantages unknown to him.

Anything I now know about Grandfather is the product of my own research—even the fact that Khorostiv was a village in Galicia (now western Ukraine) when it belonged to the Austro-Hungarian Empire. Serfdom had been abolished in 1848, but famine and cholera were regular occurrences, and the peasants' living conditions remained harsh. The Poles, who had higher social status than Ukrainians, coined an expression, *Galician misery*, that characterized the area's grinding poverty in the late 19th century.

Around the time Grandfather left Ukraine, a pamphlet for potential Ukrainian emigrants to Canada was circulating: *Pro vilni zemli* or "About Free Lands." But Grandfather missed that memo. Not only was he illiterate, he was landless.

I have chosen to tell Grandfather's story in the form of a glosa, a poem built on constraints. It begins with a four-line epigraph from Ruth Padel's "Time to Fly" and is followed by four ten-line stanzas where lines 6, 9, and 10 are end-rhymed. As required by the form, each stanza ends with a line from Padel's poem.

Grandfather

You go because you're
alive
because you're dying, maybe dead already, you go
because you must.
—Ruth Padel, "Time to Fly"

Emancipation freed you to
more readily shiver in winter,
drink vodka on credit,
doff a cap—if only you owned one—three-hundred paces
from the manor,
dodge the Pole's cudgel
and leave his mushrooms on the forest floor.
Your people own no plough—what land?
nor pig, nor cow,
and you are one mouth more.
You go because you're

fledged: no school, no work, no wife, no child,
no life past ten years more.
A skunk got in the yard but found no hens,
the millet's gone, potatoes have run out,
the cholera is back,
and bast shoes don't survive
much wet. *Galician misery* you know well.
On the steamer you finger your ikon
and pray you'll arrive
alive.

Pro vilni zemli—words that never reach your ears,
though rumours swirl of distant cream.
No mention of mines, logging camps, the sewage lines
to build. No talk of gnats or rats.
The shipping agent lends you money for the fare,
gives out the papers you must show,
and points to where you mark an X.
A hessian sack, a bony back, your name.
Your gait is slow
because you're dying, maybe dead already, you go

before the Khrystos, dank and cold,
bursts from his tomb (*Indeed he has risen*!)
and bony hips can tempt you back,
before the master's meadow greens
or fox kits leave their den,
before the sun can melt Taina's ice
and warm the banks where herons hunt by stealth.
Your lip quivers. The wagon rolls.
Not conquest, land, or wanderlust:
because you must.

Man from Trindhøj

History as battles and borders, feuds and firearms, royals and raiders—I couldn't care less. But everyday habits and circumstances? What people ate, the clothes they wore, how they threshed grain, their shelters, their gods, their rituals? Of these I can never get enough.

Man from Trindhøj

—National Museum of Denmark

Bronze-Age hands
  hewed, hollowed, and hallowed a massive oak
  and lined it with cow skin for your burial in the barrow.
You mouldered beneath buckwheat, red clover, false flax,
Beech and linden standing by.
Now only wrappings.
Blanket, tasselled and tannin stained.
Vacant tunic. Idle belt.
Cropped cope,
  warp, weft, pile, all wool.
Conical felt hat with a spare in a bark box.
One horn comb.

In the plane back to Toronto
I knit a miniature of your cape with Faroese yarn
  in linen stitch and short rows.
But, most of all,
I envied you the oak's embrace,
The solitude of the barrow.

Sounding Silence

My father was a foot soldier in World War II, belonging to the Irish Regiment of Canada. As a child I knew he had been in Italy, Belgium, and Holland during the war, and I had seen pictures of him standing in dress uniform beside my mother (his new bride) before he went overseas. But I hadn't a clue what he'd actually done as a soldier, and nobody ever talked about it. Nor was I curious.

That changed on September 3, 2020, when I received an email from a stranger.

"You probably will be surprised to receive an email from the Netherlands," the stranger wrote. "I hope it doesn't cause you any inconvenience and I hope you understand that that is not my intention."

The writer, Lieuwe Boonstra, identified himself as an amateur historian living in Heerenveen, a town liberated by Canadian forces on April 13 and 14, 1945. Members of the Irish Regiment had been billeted in his town when the war ended and before they were repatriated to Canada. Lieuwe said that he had a copy of the embarkation list of December 7, 1945, and Pte. W. Chornenki's name was on that list.

"May I ask you Madam, is Pte. W Chornenki a relative?"

Indeed. He was my father.

Lieuwe and I corresponded further. He forwarded copies of pages from the wartime journal of a local citizen and extracts from *The Story of the Irish Regiment of Canada, 1939–1945*. Reading those and other personal accounts that Lieuwe's correspondence prompted me to research, I began to glimpse—albeit faintly—the world my father had inhabited during *Operation Goldflake*. Until then, I knew nothing of the sights, smells, or sounds of "active combat," and I certainly never pictured my father lying prone with a rifle, sighting an enemy soldier.

Sounding Silence

When my father returned from the war
—the only European tour that he would ever take
crossing the Rubicon, up the Rhone, hastening to Holland—
his limbs were intact, as before,
but his dark wavy hair had been clipped to the scalp
and the mustache was gone from his lip;
his hazel eyes carried less gilding, vague mist,
as he reclaimed his everyday citizenship.
He wooed his wife with cameos brought home from Ravenna
—ladies carved in shell and girdled with gold—
and presented her with linen he'd found buried in a hole.
The baby he gave a spoon crafted of guilders,
praying that soon she would find him familiar.
He maintained discipline and good manners
where none would ask and none answer.
He sometimes said *Apeldoorn* and *Zuiderzee*,
though no one paid attention, least of all me,
the fourth of four.
I heard only the spoon clanking his coffee cup before dawn,
a goose honking into a handkerchief at Sunday Mass,
mismatched nouns and verbs,
claps of anger,
hair-trigger,
bellowing,
and blessed silence when he sat alone, his right hand
        cupping his chin.

My father was twenty years dead
before I read accounts by men who heard and felt,
men like him who saw and smelt the netherworld

where so many dwelt
—or died.
Twenty years before I read
what it was my father could never have said.
Awakened by mortar fire, half-naked,
terrific explosions, roof tiles and glass flung all around,
machine guns rattling continuously,
projectiles flaming through the air and raining down,
firing all night long without pause,
blast, fragments, leg, head,
smoke,
bridges a twisted mass of steel,
tanks with flamethrowers burning the enemy along the ditches,
sniper.
The first time in a month I took off my boots or any of my clothes.

Twenty years before I read
the wounds of war, men scarred or dead.
Mine, right leg, foot, partial amputation,
shell, chest, concussion,
shell, thigh, laceration left eye
shell, right pectoral muscles, biceps, tibia,
shell, punctured left side of skull,
shell, right thigh, leg, right shoulder, comp frac right hand, penis,
shell, amp left leg, penetrating back, chest, right arm serious.
Mourned the loss of comrades.

When my father returned from the war,
he kept his memories to himself,
like his teeth and full head of hair
—and I my distance—
until the day he died.

Kindred Spirits

Who was J.R. Hollingsworth? I have no idea, but I'm sleeping in his sheets. His name is inked on the bottom of bedding that came from at an estate auction in Hamilton, Ontario, years ago. The oversized sheets of Belgian linen are hemmed by hand at the top and embellished with drawn thread work and embroidery.

What kind of a man could afford to commission custom-made sheets and to have them laundered outside his home? I didn't initially see what Hollingsworth and I had in common.

Because I enjoy the challenge of poetic forms, when composing "Kindred Spirits" I initially adopted a discipline of six-line stanzas that repeated a specific word from the previous stanza and introduced a new one to be carried forward to the next, like so:

1. J.R. Hollingsworth,
2. straight of spine,
3. broad of chest,
4. pulled fine *linen* bedding
5. to his chin
6. at day's end.

1. Cream-coloured *linen*,
2. oh, so refined
3. subtle
4. seamless
5. French,
6. too many *threads* per inch to count.

1. Exquisite,
2. from another time
3. drawn-*thread* work,
4. by nameless hands
5. tiny warps and wefts
6. removed . . .

Ultimately, however, I amalgamated lines and shortened the stanzas. The concluding couplet presented itself to me as I walked home from an appointment at St. Michael's hospital.

Kindred Spirits

J.R. Hollingsworth, straight of spine
and broad of chest, pulled French linen bedding
to his chin at day's end.
Cream-coloured linen, so refined,
seamless and subtle,
myriad threads per square inch.
Whitework from another time
where nimble nameless fingers
plucked tiny warps and wefts,
tugged barelaid threads and silken twine
into tiny blossoms laid
in garden beds, corners set
with crosses. A superior hemline.
Posies of muted blue,
strewn on silver leaves,
to be laundered with their kind,
the family name printed
on the edge in blue ink.

Family estate sale. Sheets now mine.
Creamy linen flows over
my body at day's end
and Hollingsworth, lately confined
to a shroud, oversees my slumber
—blissful, deep and sweet.
Such repose! How disinclined
I am to rouse from liminal luxury,
to trouble myself with notifications, texts and tweets . . .

Vacant of mind, safely supine.
Softness and peace and joy and love and bliss,
the land of spices,
the bird of paradise.[2]

Remote as the man sprawled at Shuter and Bond,
COVID-19 mask still on.

Poets Considering Moss

> *The Northern Forest Region (NFR) contains over 350 mosses. The number is imprecise because mosses are small, because relatively few people study them, and because the ones that do don't agree on how many they see.*
>
> —Jerry Jenkins, *Mosses of the Northern Forest: A Photographic Guide*

Despite their obscurity and apparent insignificance, mosses may be responsible for the air we breathe and life as we know it. Computer modelling based on rocks and sea fossils proposes that, over 400 million years ago, primitive, low-growing mosses drew down carbon from the air, ultimately enabling an increase in atmospheric oxygen to today's levels, levels that sustain us humans.[3]

A pity then that so many people spend so much time trying to rid their lawns, driveways, and patio stones of moss.

Poets Considering Moss

rocks . . . threatened from underneath by moss in lovely hell-green flames

—Elizabeth Bishop, "Brazil, January 1, 1502"

afterwards I always felt mean . . . as if I had committed, against the whole scheme of life, a desecration

—Theodore Roethke, "Moss-Gathering"

August rains. Forest mosses beckon us
exactly as they must have beckoned you,
every square inch of woodland floor gone green
—frog green, hunter green, pickle green,
olive, kale and shamrock,
occasional mustards, golds and bronzes,
miniscule capsules borne on blood-red stalks.
Impossible mantle
blanketing rot and rock and soil
under spindly spruce and aspen trees
that took hold once the loggers had their way,
lining ditches where orchids bloom
in June for those who know,
hosting the cedar's seedlings, the stolons

of the wild strawberry. After rain, pure cobalt tops the trees,
poplars pulse with water,
woodpeckers tapping time—
sounds that are no sounds.
We walk, we see
how green hangs
like a tablecloth from crags
or caps a cedar stump,

shins up a living trunk
with anchor hairs concealed in matted sponge.

Still, in the foreground, blue jays squawk and scold,
insist on what is theirs, lay claims
like the bright orange ribbons
marking off the land for sale,
the luscious lot
that slopes up from the shore
with moss so green
it swallows up the honeyed sun,
so deep
it gleams all afternoon
—mustard, copper, bronze—
miniscule capsules borne on jet-black stocks.
Unbroken mantle.
Impossible.

Part 2

Lawless Law’s Enclosure

Unarmed Resistance

This poem, first submitted to a publication devoted to "the environmental crisis," received a prompt rejection.

It wasn't "joyful" enough.

Unarmed Resistance

Rumi called out, be silent and observe the world,
be a seeker of the purpose of the world.[4]

Tell me, I replied, a spoon has a purpose, a pot
—to comfort, sustain in the service of the world,

but what is to be found in the rubble and ash
where bellies are denied the surplus of the world?

I went silent, eyes wide, and what did I observe?
Roiling, boiling slag from the furnace of the world

and love poems of nightingales, ruby-clad roses
that mask darkened stains on the surface of the world.

Cast-off ruffs, red foam noses, and oversized soles
—are we naught but clowns in the circus of the world?

Master, you knew Light in the broken and absurd;
Lace my wine with opium: propose me to your world.

Empty Viking Grave, Gurness

The Vikings had a sophisticated, fourfold notion of a human being.[5]

The *hamr* was a person's outer shape or form, their container. Inside the *hamr* were a person's

- *hugr*, which roughly corresponds to the Western notion of a soul,
- *hamingja*, the personification of luck with an independent will that might, in extreme circumstances, even choose to leave the body, and
- *fylgja*, a female protector or guardian (always female) that moved down the family line at death.

In Norse mythology, dead warriors had two possible destinations, Sessrúmnir (Freyja's "Seat-Room" in the Fields of Fólkvangr) or Valhöll where Odin presided. But what is it that went anywhere on death? A warrior's *hugr* may have been what travelled, but not as a reward for a moral life (such a concept being absent in Viking thinking).

It's not known where women went when they died. Or slaves, for that matter.

Empty Viking Grave, Gurness

Easy to overlook
away as it is from ramparts and trenches
where tourists traipse and conjure broch life by the Sands
or mistake it for something fanciful,
a Neolithic bait box for limpets, say.

Her bed frame four upright slabs,
mattress of gravel,
once-upon-a-coverlet of shale,
feet to the east
and just off the shore, a roaring roost.

So little left
what with otters and waves having had their way
a thousand years
—cranium that cradles no eyes, contours no skin,
stray clavicle, lone femur.

No grave clothes, save whispers of wool
on filigreed brooches
and finespun wool it was,
she being no war booty
no thrall.

They buried her with tools for the journey north
and down
—an iron scythe to sever sinew and soul from the earth,
a knife to finish the cut.

Her soul entered Freyja's seat-room,
her luck fluttered away
and her guardian took up with kin.
But what of her *hamr*, her shape
—a deer now? a seal?

A raven
beholden to none,
least of all Odin.

The Raven on Summerhill

In some parts of the world ravens are commonplace, but not in central Toronto where I live. The city's last breeding pair were said to have been killed near the Ontario Legislative Building in 1848. For me, an urban resident with a perpetual nature deficit, seeing or even hearing a raven arouses delight.

One winter day walking east on Summerhill Avenue off Yonge Street, I heard that signature *cronk*. And there it was—a raven on the paved driveway in front of a brick house.

Before composing "The Raven on Summerhill" I analysed "The Fish" by Elizabeth Bishop (1911–1979). Then, in the manner of an art student learning how to paint sunlight on linen by copying Mary Pratt's 1987 *Bedroom*, I patterned my poem on Bishop's masterpiece.

The Raven on Summerhill

I heard a distinctive *cronk*,
stopped in mid-stride and turned.
There on a neighbour's drive—good Lord!
A raven in dark oily gear.
He didn't flinch.
He wasn't fussed at all.
He stood his ground,
a lone hunched form,
a thickset neck,
and puffed out the hackles
feathering his chest.
His beak a black forged hook,
stiff bristles on the top, beneath
the hidden nostrils
that fill with carrion stink.
But here? No rubbish bins,
just shovelled snow and pavement salt.

He shifted his leathery feet
—right left, right left—
a solemn jig in place
and fixed me with a jet eye.
Wind whipped massive scales
on his muscle-bound wings
and riffled his scapulars.
His ebony beak
parted without a sound,
gaped open, and I saw
that inside was rosewood pink,
a casket lined with silk.

I said, I thought your kind was gone
for good. The last Toronto mates
killed in 1848.
A surprise to find you now
in central downtown.

I looked into his eyes,
which were far smaller than mine
but darker, more determined,
Victorian mourning beads
sewn on bombazine,
inky obsidian
where light could barely pass.
He fastened them firm on my face,
stern, impersonal
—more like the beady orbs
of a nun searching a random sinner.
I thought, I'll bet that was you
I heard in the cemetery.
You and a mate
rending twigs for a home
—if you could call it a home—
high in the Norway spruce,
about a mile from here.
You were calling nasal *cronks*
far above the vaults and tombs
while squirrels skittered below.
It seems to me it's life
you signify, not loss and death.

The raven on the driveway stretched
his neck upward
and strained like a fisherman
pulling on a gansey
before setting out to sea.
Something red glinted,
just for a moment, speckled.
He shook his hooded head.
You do go on, he seemed to say,
as if I need to know
your every earnest thought.
You rudely interrupt me.
I have more vital things to do,
things that need not concern you.
Go now. Move on.
You've stayed here far too long.
And all the while, that rabbit carcass
—there beside your left boot—
it's started to freeze up.

City Sonnet

If a poem is written in a language other than English, I look at multiple translations to get a broader—albeit second-hand—sense of what the original evokes. So when I came across "Seaside Sonnet" by Russian poet Anna Akhmatova (1889–1966), I wondered how she had intended to open the sonnet she composed eight years before her death.

One translation began: Everything I see will outlive me . . .

Another began: It will all live longer than me . . .

Judith Hemschmeyer, who learned Russian just to be able to translate Akhmatova's poetry, offered a third option:

> Here everything will outlive me,
> Everything, even the decrepit starling houses,
> And this breeze, a vernal breeze,
> finishing its flight from across the sea.
>
> And the voice of eternity beckons
> With unearthly irresistibility,
> And over the blossoming cherry trees
> The crescent moon pours radiance . . .

Akhmatova wrote her sonnet from a summer resort town on the Gulf of Finland. I write from Toronto where twenty-eight condominium towers are slated to be built in a four-kilometer stretch of road steps from my home.

City Sonnet

Here everything will outlast us—you, me—
everything. Concrete sidewalks, asphalt roads,
these particulates, air sullied below
now venting from that subway grate.

All around us the forces of commerce
arrogate eternity: score and strip, grasp, unzip,
thrust piles to propagate fruits of the earth—
beanstalks of glass and steel.

And it seems ordained
in this gravel-grey world, no blade unturned,
that they'll always have their way.

Conquests that satiate no appetite
remind me of the racoon family
that tore down stalks, ransacked my father's corn.

After the Logging

The Bruce Peninsula, a popular hiking destination, is a 100-kilometre tongue of land poking northwest into Lake Huron. On its eastern shore above the tropical-blue waters of Georgian Bay rises a massive limestone escarpment where ferns, mosses, and thousand-year-old cedars grow.

But most trees in the Bruce are second-growth, maybe even third-growth. The forests were felled in the late 1800s and early 1900s when as many as thirty sawmills operated in the area. About 4,000 cords of hemlock and 300,000 cedar railway ties were annually shipped by train to market.[6]

After the Logging

They must have been very young when the men arrived.
Too small to arouse lust or be laid
low.
Dumb, they watched troops swing and strip,
sing and swig,
stack bodies and haul them away.

They stand now
still
stunned,
adolescents in grey gowns,
limbs entwined,
clutching each other across the trail.

Relax, girls, I want to say. *Relax.*
Spring forth
with warblers and hepatica.
But, really. How do I know
when the next man will arrive
with a chain saw and a Minister's zoning order?

The Capture

Early on the morning of April 7, 2022, Eugene Cronley surpassed the Mississippi rod-and-reel state-record for catfish, hooking a blue catfish that was five-and-a-half feet long with a girth of 41 inches and a weight of 131 lbs.

I heard all about the capture on CBC radio's *As It Happens*.

Just after 8:00 a.m., Cronley dropped a weighted line into the Mississippi River in the vicinity of Natchez, about 150 miles north of Baton Rouge. He had baited his line with stink bait—reeking pieces of skipjack herring.

Catfish can taste and smell without putting anything into their mouths. External taste receptors cover their entire bodies, especially the catlike whiskers (barbels) around the mouth. As soon as a barbel touches likely food, the catfish sucks it up like a vacuum cleaner.

"We sittin' there. Hadn't been out about two minutes then he hit it," Cronley told the interviewer. "I grabbed the pole, picked it outta the rod holder that held it, and all he kept doin' was pullin' drag. So we had to untie the boat and drift down the river with the fish."

The catfish resisted for half an hour before succumbing to exhaustion. By then, Cronley said, "I was wore out."

In Japanese folklore, catfish cause earthquakes. The Ansei Great Earthquake that shook Edo (present-day Tokyo) in 1855 is said to have occurred because the deity who supresses a giant catfish with a heavy stone was away at an assembly in western Japan.

I wrote "The Capture" in three-line stanzas of trochaic tetrameter, like Longfellow's "The Song of Hiawatha"—***By** the **shores** of **Git**chee **Gu**mee*—and after reading "The Explosion" by Philip Larkin (1922–1985). What I did not know at the time of writing was that Larkin's poem was also derivative. He described it as "my version on the Trimdon Grange Explosion," a ballad written by Thomas Armstrong in 1882 to commemorate the death of seventy-four men and boys in a mining disaster in northern England.[7] "*Don't tell a soul* where I got the idea from," Larkin wrote to his girlfriend Monica Jones.

The Capture

—after hearing Eugene Cronley of Mississippi describe how he landed a catfish the size of the poet

On the morning of his capture
light wind frisked the Mississippi,
riffling gently on her surface

where the new sun failed to pass;
down below at thirty metres
giant outlines grazed the bottom,

massive opalescent bodies
in an endless arc of forage
tasting, smelling, without sight.

One sucked in a mollusc, spit it,
sensed a clutch of shad roe, gulped it,
downed a young one of his own kind.

Vast, assured he reigned the river
throned on tires, discarded chassis,
lingered lord-like in the shadows

till he stroked a skipjack herring
—sweet compulsion swirling gently,
monarch's levy, his undoing.

I gived him to the museum,
fellow there is gonna mount him,
folks can see him now for always.

Of a sudden—pain and peril;
lurching downstream in a frenzy
tethered to a spectral rival

he became a maddened warrior,
a persistent pulsing fury;
tortured moments, each eternal.

On the morning of his capture
when he met death on the river
newsreels said that Edo trembled.

Such was the force of life in him.

Night Sky

It was August 14, 2003, just past 4 p.m. More than 50 million North Americans—including most Ontarians—found themselves without electrical power. Toronto's subways, traffic lights, and elevators stopped working, and its cell phones and computer screens went dark for hours and hours.

During the blackout, my friend Rebecca and her children lay on blankets in the backyard, staring up at the night sky.

"Wow! I didn't know Toronto had stars," her son exclaimed.

Night Sky

The Romantics were wrong about it.
How well they conjured sparks, eternal space,
how well they lit flares of light, steadfast bright,
a million million billions.
How even the chaste Hopkins waxed orgasmic,
Look at the stars! look, look up at the skies!

They never divined
the measure by which diurnal dark would disappear
—tugged by the steam engine—
and with it the stars.
In *Café, le soir*, for instance, how convincingly Vincent
splatters them
like bugs on glass,
permanently pasted in the sky over the terrace
where we nurse absinthe and ponder the Baths of Constantine.

But none of us see such sky, such stars,
none in cities
where the night is bright
with street lights and headlights, porch lights and spotlights,
blue light.
Where a young man steps into traffic,
lost in a luminous lure.
His grandfather said stars once peppered the night sky
but to him they are product ratings.

What Now, Patricia?

For me, to read a poem is to engage in a private conversation; the poet speaks, and I respond: *Lovely.* Or, *That's a novel way of putting it.* Or, *I have absolutely no idea what you are talking about!*

Even better are explicit conversations that poets have with each other by means of their art, that long history of response poetry. In 2007, Scottish poet Carol Ann Duffy edited *Answering Back: Living poets reply to the poetry of the past*, an anthology in which contemporary poets answered poets of their choice—Dylan Thomas, Edna St. Vincent Millay, Gerrard Manley Hopkins, Elizabeth Bishop, and others.

"What Now Patricia" is my response to "Planet Earth," by Canadian poet P.K. Page (1916–2010). Almost twenty-five years ago, the United Nations adopted Page's poem in an attempt to encourage global dialogue about climate change.

Page was a poet of great skill and depth, but her gentle injunctions now seem to me naïve, what with the disappearance of Iceland's Okjökuul glacier and the sinking of Tuvalu into the Pacific Ocean:

> It has to be loved the way a laundress loves her linens,
> the way she moves her hands caressing the fine muslins
> knowing their warp and woof,
> like a lover coaxing, or a mother praising . . .

What Now, Patricia?

—the day William Shatner went to space

Your love note to Gaia, elegant epistle,
Ribbons of reverence, silk streams of praise.
You want us to bless her, to dress and caress her,
To genuflect, cherish, in so many ways.

But we don't, Patricia. We won't.

We scour her as if she's a badly scorched pot.
We root up her cresses, toss cans in her streams,
We scrape up her seabeds, we drive SUVs.

And the sky, blazoned blue, O! O! O! overhead?
Abraded by men of affairs with machines,
Competing to outdo her song with their dreams.

What now, Patricia? What now?

Veriditas

When the World Health Organization declared COVID-19 a pandemic in March 2020, all of Canada's provinces and territories imposed states of emergency. Lockdowns were mandated, and daily life curtailed. With unstructured time on our hands, many of us turned our attention to nature, to things like wild flowers, puddles, or spider webs, things that had always been available to us.

Out walking one day my husband overheard this conversation:

"Listen. Did you hear that? I think it's a cardinal."

"What? You mean different birds make different sounds?"

Veridititas

—Mount Pleasant Cemetery, Easter 2020

While we hoard and huddle at home,
harrowed by a virus that wears a crown of thorns,
sporadically happy, intermittently holy,
light-spun myrrh bearers waken the earth
with quickening psalms and catalogues of clamour:
  tweets, peeps, bells, chirps,
   whistles, whinnies, trills,
    nasal notes and honks,
     sometime-shrieks and squawks.
Rousing the oak on the crest of the hill,
high in the pine to the right,
left on the leafless lilac.
Spilling from sepulchres, crosses, and stones.

A meet Magdalene message: the beloved lives.

Free Radicals

A growing body of research shows that exposure to nature—non-man-made places like parks or greenspaces—can improve a person's overall mood and refresh or revive mental functioning.[8] But those of us confined to cities don't always have ready or unimpeded access to the living world's restorative sights and sounds. We must be attentive—and lucky—if we are to witness nature's intermittent appearances.

Free Radicals

1.

Amid roaring trucks, giraffe-neck cranes,
all-day hammering, bicycle lanes,
curbside cafés where waiters pour wine
and teenagers hunch over takeout,
a hoarse screech.
There! Way up there!
Two hawks.
Hey! Two more!
High in the haze, spiralling.
Eight beats, two apiece.
Gone.

2.

Cued for carbohydrate
the eye craves more
—and, lo!
Towers of steel part to reveal
puffs of purest white,
cumulus billows, cumulus pillows
transfiguration lit.

3.

Past a building site with ground scraped bare,
jets overhead churning worn air,
curb waiters filling more glasses with wine,
hydro trucks parked on the pavement.
A quadrangle of sneezeweed, woman-tall,
and grey-headed coneflower bustling with bees.
Bees!

Never mind the monarchs.
Whoever saw so many urban bees, foraging, fuzzing?
Winged giants with black rumps and bumpers of pollen.
Bumblebees savouring, hovering.
Honey bees with long striped bellies.
Wee bees.
Humming in tune with traffic.

4.

Farther up Yonge Street
on the sidewalk at Jackes Avenue,
a scatter of baby dills,
shattered glass.

One Heart

English poet John Clare (1793–1864) was enchanted by the natural world. He loved tramping about, botanizing, and birding, and his poems detail rural life in the eastern flatlands of England where he was born. Clare's poetry laments humanity's impact on nature, and he identified the Anthropocene two-hundred years before the term was invented.

Between 1809 and 1820, the British Parliament privatized the commons. Local landowners were allowed to fence off fields, rivers, marshes, and forests—even Swordy Well, an ancient Roman quarry—excluding members of the public who had grazed cattle, celebrated the changing seasons, or simply rambled in those places. Because he needed the work, Clare joined teams of men felling trees and fencing fields, even as he documented the destruction in poems such as "The Moors."

> Each little tyrant with his little sign
> Shows where man claims, earth glows no more divine
> . . . And birds and trees and flowers without a name
> All sighed when lawless law's enclosure came.

I found Clare's poetry to be charming and sentimental—until I read his work more carefully and learned about his life and times, including his mental breakdown. Now I recognize the extent to which Clare captures my own impotence and sorrow at the relentless degradation of the natural world. "One Heart" is, therefore, deceptively cheerful. It evolved from a morning visit to the Don Valley Brickworks Park, a reclaimed clay quarry forty-minutes' walk from my home.

"One Heart" is a rondeau, the disciplined form that John McCrae adopted for his famous poem "In Flanders Fields."

One Heart

—Don Valley Brickworks Park

The quarry lives, my dear John Clare.
Like Swordy Well men scraped her bare,
hauled clay for bricks from far below
where neither reed nor vole could grow.
Their cart wheels wrought a thoroughfare.

But time and tending make repair.
Now waters pool, wild roses flare,
a hawk drops on a heedless hare.
The quarry lives.

No fence or sentry posted there
halt beavers when they hew their share.
I saw their work, blonde chips below
a pointed stump, the tree laid low,
and cheered on your behalf, dear Clare.
The quarry lives!

The Redress of Nature

One summer day I walked the Annapolis Valley dykelands from Wolfville Harbour to Port Williams. No other hikers were present, and the dykes were magnificent, rampant with grasses and sedges in full bloom.

> . . . I am very fond of grass, I always have been,
>   but there must
> Be no cow, person or house to be seen.
>
> Sea and grass must be quite empty.
> Other souls can find somewhere *else*.
>
> —Stevie Smith (1902–1971) "Scorpion."

Two weeks later, when I returned, the dykes had been mown. The grasses and sedges—their lush blades and pendulous flowers once so elegant—were dry, brittle, and prostrate.

The Redress of Nature

Pity the sow in the farrowing crate
restrained,
contained,
not allowed to be
her genuine she, nursing free.

Luckless the grass in suburban yards
chopped,
cropped,
never windblown
or left alone, endlessly mown.

But on the verge of the farmer's field
where feral hogs
root and ravage soybeans
—an ecstasy of blooming grasses.

Part 3

If I Were God

Highland Dithyramb

I pick my way along the Inver River in north-west Scotland, and James McBride's memoir comes to mind. The one about the white, Jewish mother who told her bi-racial son, "God is the color of water. Water doesn't have a color."

No colour?

Tell that one to the river.

Highland Dithyramb

Let us consider the great I AM
who features in flames and commands from clouds
Forbids ought but him as maker and master
Racks woman and snake—the severest of fathers.
But in Assynt?
In Assynt, she is oatmeal roiling in a steely grey pot,
coffee and burnt sugar,
minty milk,
purpled kale shouting into the wind,
Lewisian Gneiss set firm.
And all the many things that amuse her:
tree lungwort and beard lichen,
blueberries, blackberries, sloes,
the inky blue of a mussel shell, its opaline interior,
a stalking grey heron.
The places where she lets herself be named—
Kirkaig, Culag, Traligill, Loch Inver.

Fall Morning Canticle

Fully awake, eyes wide open, the medieval mystic Hildegard of Bingen (1098-1179) trembled at the "heavenly light" she witnessed from the age of three onward. Out of fear she kept the experiences to herself until the year 1141:

> And behold, in the forty-third year of my passing course, while I was intent upon a heavenly vision with great fear and tremulous effort, I saw a great splendor, in which a voice came from heaven saying to me: "O weak mortal, both ash of ash and rottenness of rottenness, say and write what you see and hear . . . speak the things you see and hear; and write them not according to yourself or any other person, but according to the will of the One Who knows, sees, and disposes all things in the hidden places of his mysteries.

Thereafter, and as commanded, Hildegard recorded her visions in words, music, and images—stars, showers of light, wavy lines, orbs, mandalas, winged creatures, clothed and unclothed bodies, and other wondrous things.

Like Hildegard, I pay close attention to and treasure what I see. At the age of forty, I too experienced light: a clear, bright central orb with mist at the periphery, dark wavy lines, and a thick, straight line off to one side. But I was not having a mystical experience. The strange sightings signalled a retinal detachment in my left eyeball, a sight-threatening condition.

Fall Morning Canticle

Hildegard said to me,
the light that I see
is not spatial
yet it is far brighter than a cloud
surrounding the sun.

And I replied,
the light that *I* see
is honey,
boundless amber and topaz.
Far from its source in the east
it speaks with clarity to the maples
and ministers to their shadows on the path.
Neither cloud nor mist,
gilding the rose hips.

O generosa, October sun!
Blessèd be.

The Burning Bin

"I don't get it," Lynn said. "I don't get the poem on page 211."

Those of us in a poetry study group were reading *The Penguin Book of the Prose Poem*, edited by Jeremy Noel-Tod. "Goodtime Jesus" had Lynn stumped:

> . . . Take a little ride on my donkey, I love that donkey. Hell, I love everybody.

"Lynn, it's a parody."

"Oh."

The Burning Bin

Just as Maurice reached the intersection, a nearby city waste bin burst into flames. Holy Shit, he said. He'd been meditating on the world's sorrows, all those smitten or in captivity—Yazidis, Uighurs, Rohingya . . . Who could they turn to? Who could relieve their suffering? Lula, Pope Francis, Guterres, Thunberg? He shook his head and fingered his prayer beads now hot to the touch.

Fire! someone shouted, Fire!

A police cruiser roared up and an officer jumped out, yanking the pin from a fire extinguisher and letting loose with the spray. Whoosh! The fire rumbled and the flames leapt even higher.

Now look at that, Maurice said. I must turn aside and see this great sight, why the bin is not burnt—an accelerant, perhaps? But the heat was too intense and the fire smelled like charred pickles. He averted his face, shielded it with his baseball cap. Should he take off his shoes?

He'd no sooner touched the lace on his right runner than a voice barked, Stand back! Stand back and move on!

Maurice bristled. There was no call for rudeness. Moreover, he wasn't ready to move on. What about the people? he wanted to know. My sisters and brothers? All those swilling in the vast sea of suffering? He waited for a sign, patient in the heat and fumes while the voice coughed and made horking sounds.

Tell me, Maurice finally rasped, show me, please! But all he heard were crackles and sizzles.

He stood until his face and hands felt quite crisped up, then turned away. Bugger off, he said over his shoulder. I'm glad I didn't trouble to take off my shoes.

Maurice waited for the light to change and walked on to the grocery store. He visited the dairy section, then went looking for a clerk. Where do I find honey? he asked.

For Halima

Impotence isn't just a medical condition that worries men. It's a contemporary state of mind, a distemper, a powerlessness that can afflict anyone. We may have personal agency, but we can do nothing to alter the state of the world.

Rather than experience hopelessness, many of my friends amuse themselves with movies, works of fiction, and humorous social media posts. They shun the daily news.

I don't want to anesthetize myself like that.

"For Halima" is a villanelle, the poetic form that Dylan Thomas chose for "Do Not Go Gentle into That Good Night" and Elizabeth Bishop chose for "One Art." It seems an appropriate form for contemplating world events; as Mark Strand and Elizabeth Boland write, the villanelle "circles around and around, refusing to go forward in any kind of linear development."[9]

For Halima

I ask you friends, please don't avert your eyes.
Heed what ancient olive trees feel and see,
and pray for the means to salve the wounds, the cries.

No chance to bid her flocks, her fields goodbye,
so up above the table hangs a key.
I ask you friends, please don't avert your eyes.

Her plate of beans was laid out when the skies
exploded concrete, metal, dust, debris.
Oh, for the means to salve the wounds, the cries!

Sons, fathers, husbands squat with burning thighs.
No Shem, Japheth to veil their nudity.
I ask you friends, please don't avert your eyes.

White winding sheets, black lettering, string ties.
Four generations lost for all eternity.
Oh, for the means to salve the wounds, the cries.

The one who hears world sighs, does she take sides?
Or does the one who bids, come follow me?
I ask you, friend, please don't avert your eyes.
Had I the means, I'd soothe all wounds, all cries.

Urban Air

In a world that tolerates so much ambient noise, it amused me to learn that the Salvation Army's Christmas bell-ringing prompted noise complaints.

Urban Air

Moaning mower, Leaf Blower!
chopper thwap-thwap-thwapping over

Construction site, clanging clamour
jack-jack-jack-jack-jack-jackhammer

Thumping Bass, pornographic
thrumming-thrumming-thrumming traffic

Peck-peck, pick-pick, keypad entry
faux Alexa standing sentry

System haptics, cyborgs next
email whoosh
buzz buzz text

Ring, ping, bong, gong, click, clack, frick, frack. . . .

Yogurt with Strains of Sogdian

No! I do not have a yogurt maker.

I have a stainless steel pot from Ikea, an OXO analog instant read thermometer, an induction cook top, and an oven. I heat eight cups of milk to 180 degrees Fahrenheit, cool it down to between 90 and 100 degrees, stir in the remains of the last batch of yogurt, and incubate the inoculated milk—still in its budget pot—overnight inside an oven warmed to 125 degrees. The next morning I put the pot into the refrigerator until I have time to ladle the yogurt into large Weck jars with "Fresh Cover" lids.

Yogurt with Strains of Sogdian

According to chef Batmanglij,
yogurt comes from
an old branch

of Persian, streaming
its way
out of Turkey

to colonize guts
in the west.
Now

wholesome from cows
treasured
like children,

letting down with love
hormone-free
milk set

with probiotics, no
faux flavours
fructose

fruit or preservatives.
Sold in
plastic containers.

Botanizing with Vladimir

Dostoyevsky's *The Brothers Karamazov* was challenging to read. So many characters! What I didn't understand was that *Alyosha*, *Alyoskka*, *Alyoshenka*, *Alyoshechka*, *Alexeichik*, *Lyosha*, and *Lyoshenka* all refer to the same person—Alexei Fyodorovich Karamazov. Those names are diminutives, terms of endearment (and sometimes of insult) used by family and friends. And *Fyodorovich* is a patronymic indicating the Alexei is the son of Fyodor.

"Botanizing with Vladimir" invites Vladimir Vladimirovich Putin to consider how the wild strawberry claims territory: it sends out a slender, exploratory thread and produces a tiny rosette that puts down roots only after the thread touches the ground.

Russians call the wild strawberry *zemlyanika*, a word that combines *zemlya* (earth) and *nika* (to bow).

Botanizing with Vladimir

Look, Volodya,
how the wild strawberry
launches an umbilical cord
wine dark and wire sturdy
straight from its heart;
makes a miniature of itself,
elfin leaves
the tiniest of trinities held up on downy stalks
nestled in blades of timothy.

Here, Voloden'ka,
one is blooming
—five virgin petals,
a crown in the centre
enlisting honey bees that pollinate the buckwheat and the rye,
tempting cuckoo bees that pirate other nests.
And over there,
a scarlet berry gone from green to white to ripe,
an offering, a prayer.

Taste, Volodya,
place it on your tongue
and feel its force, the concentrated sun,
the shocking sweetness of that tiny bead.
Did you help your mother harvest berries for jam
in sun-filled meadows beyond the dacha
on the way to the river?
Woman's work, yes,
so much bending to fill a bowl.

Zemlyanika, those berries.
The way they hang,
the way they weigh the stalks down to the ground
where waxwings, starlings
dip to feed,
where chipmunks, badgers, even foxes
bend and browse.
Foxes, Vladimir Vladimirovich,
even foxes bow their heads.

If I were God

Misophonia—literally, hatred of sound—is a little-studied condition in which certain sounds provoke intense emotional reactions and involuntary physical responses such as disgust, rage, or panic.

"I think this is us," my friend Carol emailed, including a link to an article on the subject.

In Carol's case, human sounds like chewing, slurping, or sniffing set her off. In my case, repetitive mechanical noises torment me.

If I were God

I would exceed Artemis of Ephesus with her necklace of knackers
and the handmaid of the Lord, Great Mother though she be.
I would be pitiless,
punishing to those who desecrate the primal void and shatter my
sacred silence.
Nuclear.
Fierce.
Conjuring a cube from which no peep or plea escapes.
Confined, their blood as dust, their flesh as dung,
The Mustang Mach 1 driver, bursting bass notes pounding,
thudding, throbbing
buildings on both sides.
The morning walker yelling at a cell phone: *Do you know how*
hot it is in Portugal in June?
He with the two-stroke leaf blower.
Hydraulic hammers shuddering Scrivener Square.
Idling dump trucks queued on Yonge Street.
Real estate developers from Vaughan.
Juvenile tuba practice through the plasterboard.
I would wall them in together and let them roar
Roar and roar and roar
Roar beyond demented
Roar forevermore.

Open Letter to Meng Wanzhou

What would it be like to have the unjust imprisonment of two men on your conscience?

On December 1, 2018, Meng Wanzhou, deputy chair of the board of directors of Huawei, was arrested at Vancouver's International Airport at the request of the United States. The arrest was made pursuant to an extradition treaty between Canada and the United States where Meng was charged with fraud and conspiracy to commit fraud in order to circumvent U.S. sanctions against Iran. Days later and by way of retaliation, two Canadians, Michael Kovrig and Michael Spavor, were arrested and jailed in China. They each spent almost three years living in tiny, crowded cells where the lights were always on, allowed few phone calls and no consular visits.[10]

By contrast, Meng was released on bail within days of her arrest and lived in luxury in Vancouver while a team of lawyers fought the extradition request in Canadian courts. On the first anniversary of her arrest, Meng addressed "netizens" in a lyrical open letter. The letter (since removed) was posted on Huawei's website under the heading **Your warmth is a beacon that lights my way forward**:

> With winter approaching, I can see the dense forests begin to slowly turn the hills around me to a deep crimson . . . Right now, time seems to pass slowly. It is so slow that I have enough time to read a book from cover to cover. I can take the time to discuss minutiae with my colleagues or to carefully complete an oil painting . . . Every single encouragement spoken has motivated me to read one more book or take one more course.

The letter was signed "Sabrina Meng." *Sabrina*? Interesting choice. Sabrina is a water goddess who lives in the Severn River that flows through England and Wales, and she has the power to rescue maidens in danger.

There *was* something of the goddess about Meng Wanzhou. Photographs taken on the steps of a British Columbia court house in May 2020 show a definite resemblance to Guanyin, the bodhisattva of boundless compassion depicted in Song dynasty statues and paintings. Guanyin is she who hears and responds to the cries of the world.

When several prominent Canadians urged Canada's Minister of Justice to end extradition proceedings against Meng in order to free Michael Kovrig and Michael Spavor, I invoked Meng instead. While some say she lacked agency in the matter, I maintain that she could easily have freed the men by surrendering to authorities in the United States and defending herself in that country.

Open Letter to Meng Wanzhou

There is a gentle nymph not far from hence,
That with moist curb sways the smooth Severn stream.
Sabrina is her name, a virgin pure.

—John Milton, *Comus*, 1634

I read your post to netizens,
the one you signed "Sabrina."
Your heartfelt prose perplexes me
Is that how you wish us to see you?
  Sentient sprite splashing the Severn
  grand robes afloat, rippled reflection
  safely indulging all nature's perfection.
  Bathed in opulence, time your treasure,
  savouring books from cover to cover.
(Have you read *The Two Michaels* by Kovrig and Spavor?)
Watching the seasons green, glow, and fade
be mindful, Meng, you have the power to save.
Hear them, Sabrina, hear them and save:
  renounce your reflection
  admit your connection
  advance their protection
Hear them and save.
On the steps of the courthouse
you change to Guanyin
regal demeanor, porcelain skin
cupid bow mouth, deftly arched brow
Why is it you hid such perfection till now?
Most gracious goddess, mercy your measure
  do you hear the sighs of the men as they suffer?
  the lonely despairing of Kovrig and Spavor?
Recall what the sutra says about you

that one invocation will save a ship's crew
tossing and turning on violent seas.
I beg, Bodhisattva, grant them your favour:
reverse your direction
forego your objection
relieve their subjection
Hear them and save.

Consular Visit

To:
Michael Kovrig
Beijing No. 1 Detention Centre
501 Dougezhuang County, Chaoyang District, Beijing
100021
The People's Republic of China

To:
Michael Spavor
Dandong Detention Centre
Jingu Village, Zhenxing District
Dandong, Liaoning Province
118000
The People's Republic of China

In June 2021, I mailed a copy of "Consular Visit" to each of Michael Kovrig and Michael Spavor using the jail addresses I found for them on the internet. I do not know whether they ever received my poem.

Consular Visit

—for Michael Kovrig and Michael Spavor, Don Valley Brickworks Park

You and I sit together in the quarry
where life replenishes
what once was taken away.
Currents of air wisp our forearms, feather our faces.
Unmown grass and unbound green summon,
soothe
sight.
We breathe
deep
sweet sweat of flowering locust trees.
Purple martins rattle and whistle.
Green frogs pulse time in a water lily pond,
slow-paced,
spaced,
cell walls erased.

What You Won't See Can't Hurt You

> *Garbage. I started thinking about what happens to all the garbage. I mean, where do we put all of it? We have to run out of places to put it eventually, don't we?*
>
> —Ann Bishop Mullaly in "Sex, Lies, and Videotape"

This scene from Steven Soderbergh's 1989 movie came to mind as I walked one of Toronto's tony neighbourhoods in springtime. It was early on a Wednesday morning, municipal garbage day. Dozens of discards, often in working order, awaited pickup.

While walking I played Kim's Game, memorizing in reverse order the garbage piles I passed.

What You Won't See Can't Hurt You

I went for a walk in a neighbourhood
of mullioned windows and ancient oaks
on garbage day in May,
and I saw
a busted fibreglass snow sled propped against the curb.
A snow sled and a disassembled child's bed: headboard,
footboard, slats.
A sled, a bed, and white plastic shelving never unpacked.
A sled, a bed, pristine plastic, and a patio table
smeared with winter grime.

One ivory damask pedestal chair,
gold foam poking through a tear on the arm.
One pedestal chair and three once-white dining room chairs,
oak legs in the air.
One pedestal chair, three legs-in-the-air chairs, two metal
ironing boards clutching each other,
no padded covers.

A green garden hose
coiled like a snake.
A hose and a metal rooster clanking on a pole.
A hose, a rooster, and a haystack of hoes, rakes, and shovels in
working order.

A bar fridge
closed tight.
A bar fridge and a gleaming glass coffee maker in an open
cardboard box.

A fridge, a coffee maker, and a mangy pvc push broom on a blue
metal broomstick.
A frameless mirror partially wrapped in paper and painter's tape.

A pair of boy's skates,
yellow laces knotted together.
Skates and a trio of hockey sticks laid flat on grass cut
military style.
Skates, hockey sticks, and a walnut coffee table on its back,
legs removed and trussed beside it.

And upright on sidewalks
by travertine driveways,
bulging leaf bags
folded closed.
Cardboard boxes
flattened and bundled with string.
240-litre garbage bins on wheels, spilling white packing foam.
Recycling bins brimming with takeout containers.
Compost bins, bound with bungee cords.

Two trucks
rumbling in from opposite directions
whisked it all away.

After Wordsmithing

"Take out the function words." At least once every poetry class, a fellow student repeated that injunction.

"Take out the function words."

Why? On whose authority?

Function words serve a purpose. They indicate grammatical or structural relationships among words in a sentence, and a poem, according to Thomas C. Foster, is really just one or more sentences.

To challenge the rule adopted by my classmates, I analysed several well-known poems, including Robert Frost's "After Apple-Picking." By my count, twenty-five percent of the words Frost used in his poem were function words:

- 25 determiners—*the, a, that, my, more, much, either, neither*
- 13 conjunctions—*and, that, when, while, although, or*
- 19 prepositions—*of, at, in, without, between, to, after*
- 10 pronouns—*he, they, anybody, it, one, myself*
- 7 particles—*no, not, nor, as*, and
- 5 auxiliaries—*is, am, are, have, got, do.*

In writing "After Wordsmithing" I had fun matching the line lengths and metre Frost used in "After Apple-Picking."

After Wordsmithing

My long well-sharpened pencil's scraping cross the page
Where letters spill,
And there's a coffee cup I didn't fill
Beside it, and there may be two or three
Light function words I left in anyhow,
For I embrace what today's poets disavow.
Determiners, conjunctions can sit right,
Those hints of grammar wrought with ease by Frost
Whose apple-picking poem imparts delight
And tallies tiny words at minor cost.
I scanned his poem for prepositions too
Then took out all the function words I found.
It weakened, and its walls fell to the floor.
But I was glad
To see how it revived were I to add
What once it had.
An exercise that seems to underscore
Most cherished rules are dogma, nothing more.

Chorus of Entitlement

A friend's sister had ocular melanoma. The oncologist called her response to treatment "spectacular." But her luck gave out. When tumours returned, she explained to her university class that she would be away during their final exams in order to start a new treatment regime. Then, unbeknownst to her, a student went to administration to complain about the word *cancer.*

And so, this poem began.

Then, I couldn't get stopped. Everywhere I turned, I encountered humanity's selfabsorption and indifference to the suffering of others—even from a road racer whose vehicle landed on my sister's front lawn after he killed another motorist.

Recently, I read this poem at the book launch of a fellow poet. (She specifically requested it.) As I told the crowd, I didn't make any of these examples up.

Chorus of Entitlement

—insights from W.H. Auden (1907–1973)

Sung in the lecture hall

So sorry, class.
I won't be there to invigilate your exam.
My cancer treatments start that day.
What about me? cried the girl in faux-poor jeans
tweeting her latest distress.
My feelings affected,
pain resurrected,
neurosis connected.
I won't hear that word!
The academy conferred
Then gave its answer:
Never say *cancer*
in front of a class.

Sung on the radio

So sorry, listeners.
Our guest says you've ravaged the sea,
filled it with man-made debris.
Plastic waste intensifying,
whales entangled, seabirds dying,
lame excuse to say you're trying.
Give up that single-use bag.
What about me? sighed the woman with the toddler
who was that day's second caller.
I need plastic bags for groceries
to transport home our cookies
and my Keurig coffee pods.
Cloth bags are too heavy.

I can't lift and carry
unless it's petroleum made.

Sung at the airport

So sorry, travellers.
Max 8 aircraft down,
passengers hurtled from high.
Families reeling, grieving, keening.
The jets won't fly authorities say
and this will cause you some delay.
What about me? vied the teacher, departing Orlando.
I now must drive two-hundred miles,
rent a car,
go so far.
Without compensation I've no consolation.
What, oh what, about me?

Sung under pressure

So sorry, motorists.
Atmosphere warming
noxious clouds forming.
Cars cause congestion, impair respiration,
a clear correlation.
Use transit or walk.
What about me? tried the man with the Burberry raincoat
who drives to his tower downtown.
The subway has faces
from populous places;
they're going to displace us
and I catch their germs.
I was ill without warning
from transit this morning.

Sung from Etobicoke

So sorry, diners.
The virus is shedding
pandemic is spreading
No meetings, no weddings,
no in-person meals.
Follow me! the pied piper of barbeque called
who was fined when he kept selling ribs.
My lockdown citation's
a form of castration,
the worst degradation
a man could endure.
To spread an infection
my rights need protection.
If you fund my fight, I'll set the world right.

Sung with indifference

So sorry, road racer,
you're fatal when fast.
Your van was a lethal machine in your hands,
even more when you taunted a nearby sedan
and someone else paid with a shortened lifespan.
What about me? plied the one with a crumpled fender
who just killed an innocent man.
The dead need no mention
It's me needs attention,
with my hypertension
I'm in urgent need.

The torturer's horse still scratches its innocent behind on a tree
as Icarus tumbles through space.
An unimportant failure.

Part 4

The Eternal Return

No time, like the present

> *Archaeology is a highly interpretive undertaking, a constant balancing of probabilities and alternatives.*
>
> —Neil Price, *Children of Ash and Elm*

My oldest brother was days away from death when I learned he was in palliative care in Grand Forks, British Columbia. He had instructed his spouse to tell no one until he had died. But as the end drew closer, she countermanded his instructions and reached out to my sister.

How to make sense of my brother's secrecy? He and I kept in touch by email (granted, periodically), but there'd been no hint—not the least whisper—of any sort of trouble. His correspondence had been cogent and upbeat, and we'd exchanged thoughts on current events, including the situation in Gaza and the November 2024 US election.

No time, like the present

What do you say to a man who is dying
two-thousand miles away,
whose words were artifacts
even before they swept grasslands and boreal forests
on their way to you:
Things are going well. As a matter fact, I couldn't have planned them better,
except perhaps for want of a Bentley in the garage,
but let's not get carried away,
who said that each morning he made his bed, washed his bowl and got on with his day:
Ah, no time like the present!
while holding his breath under the quilt,
convinced no one would find him there?

What do you say when you dial his number
and the phone rings and rings and rings?
You rehearse, praying that he will answer,
hoping that he won't.

A cord stretches long, long, and a voice pulls through batting.
Hello! is what you say next.

Do you chide him for launching another solo adventure?
Tell him you saw a hawk in the city sky that sounded like a seagull?
Ask him how his garden fares in the drought?

A pulse of bleeps—
Hello? Hello? Are you still there?

You dial again.
Voice mail.

It's me, your baby sister.
Just calling to say goodbye.

The Joyful Wisdom

As an eighteen- or nineteen-year-old I was a keen and reflective reader. I filled a hard-cover notebook with extracts from the classics and copied sayings from Ovid, Erasmus, St. Augustine, Martin Buber, and Nietzsche.

Nietzsche? Really?

Yes, but I didn't realize that *amor fati* and *eternal return* consigned me to perpetual boredom.

The Joyful Wisdom

I dreamt once that I was condemned to death
not by hanging or chair,
but by a formless darkness deep inside.
Confirmed.
No known repair.
As I recall, I feared not nothingness
nor unremitting pain,
but pulsed and ached as I walked the park
—I'd not see the maples leaf again
or kick their hundred, hundred keys
abandoned on the path.

Longer.
Slower.
Later, please.
Let time be a circle, a rotating wheel,
a wandering line to the place it began,
caressing each fragment and blessing the bad:
  the thieving employer,
  those unrequited loves,
  my loneliest loneliness,
  airport pickpocket,
  seven stitches in my left eyeball.

Was that life? I will say to death.
Very well! Once more!

On waking, I remember that Nietzsche's eternal return
means life, in the same
series and sequence,
numberless times.

Born to Atone

At the end of 2023, I sat in on a course about the Book of Psalms. I say "sat in on" because, while I always appreciate learning about ancient poetry and songs, I was distracted by the content. I could not fathom the group's enthusiasm for the personal god addressed in the psalms, the one that takes sides. All I could think about were bombs dropping on civilians, and that god was—where?

In the final session, participants were invited to write their own psalm using a prescribed template. Let me at it, I said. But I could not follow the template.

For a prompt, I chose Psalm 22: *My God, my God, why hast thou forsaken me?* That phrase reappears in the New Testament as the anguished cry of a crucified man, an adult who, despite his cry, accepted death. That death has since been interpreted as a willing sacrifice on behalf of the world. "Born to Atone" is a parallel passage written for the present day.

Born to Atone

—Al-Shifa Hospital, 2023

My God, she is forsaken.
None intercedes on her behalf.
The Pontius Pilates wash their hands
and do not even ask, what evil has she done?
See ye to it is their silent chant.

Fresh from the womb scarce taken,
transparent manger for a bed,
her term abrupt. So small
and yet no comfort on her mother's shrivelled breast;
an early taste of vinegar with gall.

Her people cower, shaken,
poured like water though none be,
nor food nor light nor heat.
Her brother whimpers, will my toys still be alive?[11]
Her cross of girders, smoke and dust, concrete.

The Pontius Pilates wring their hands,
and do not dare to ask, what evil has she done?
See ye to it still their wordless chant.

And what of he, the Liege Lord of creation
who thrusts the cup into wee fists
unable to say no?
May generations hold him to account on her behalf,
reproach the unearned suffering he imposed.

Things We're Not Meant to Understand

Butterflies and snakes have mythological significance—as intermediaries, as images of transformation, rebirth, mystic knowledge . . .

But what about a butterfly *on* a snake?

"Mythology cannot be rationally understood," Joseph Campell wrote.[12] "Theological interpreters render it ridiculous, and literary criticism reduces it to metaphor."

Things We're Not Meant to Understand

Why a butterfly tiptoes along a snake,
follows its yellow stripes like a gymnast
on a balance beam, stroking each scale.
A dead garter flattened clay-dry,
meeting truck wheels before it reached the verge.
Down for days, dismissed by coyotes and crows
but compelling to a white admiral
caressing its corpse with wings as a Faroese shawl.

Why the butterfly drops to ground
and spins in the coils of the dead body,
then remounts, mincing towards the tail.

Why a woman eases her bony frame off a gurney
robe trailing behind, eyes towards the door.
My train, she says, they're calling my train.

Wish for Her

Marija Gimbutas (1921–1994) was a controversial archeologist and folklorist who did not believe that prehistoric art and religion were inscrutable. She studied the signs and design patterns preserved in Neolithic Europe's artifacts which comprised a complex system of interlocking units, and, in her professional opinion, these indicated that at one time the same Goddess religion was common to the Near East, southeastern Europe, the Mediterranean area, and in central western and northern Europe. Disturbances and incursions by a very different Neolithic culture which Gimbutas called "Kurgan" (*kurgan* meaning "barrow" in Russian) put an end to Old European culture between 4300 and 2800 BCE transforming it into a patriarchal, militaristic culture.

In the introduction to *The Language of the Goddess*, Gimbutas wrote:

> We are still living under the sway of that aggressive male invasion and only beginning to discover our long alienation from our authentic European Heritage—gylanic, nonviolent, earth-centred culture.

Twenty-first century readers may find that assertion to be fanciful or idealistic, placing females in a superior position and dissing males. But the Wife of Bath whom Chaucer developed in the late fourteenth century seems to have shared Gimbutas's attitude:

> Who peyntede the leon, tel me who?
> By God, if wommen hadde writen stories,
> As clerkes han withinne hire oratories
> They wolde han writen of men moor wikkednesse
> Than al the mark of Adam may redresse.[13]

Wish for Her

In the name of the maiden, mother, crone
the opening words resound, and all knees bend
in boundless mist, all eyes and ears attend
eight sirens spiralling the spindle stone
each weaving into harmony her tone;
weft music few of us can apprehend.
Yet, undeterred, they hymn again, again
—behold, The One, Great Goddess, on her throne!

Why is it now that dust motes strew her bones?
Her wholeness whittled down to harlot, wife,
rebellious teeth in apples seeding strife?
Who silenced She who governed death and life?

Who painted the lion? Alisoun knew.
If only my mother had known it too.

The Lucky Ones

When a former boyfriend's sister died, I emailed him my condolences. "Ah," he replied, "I see you've taken to reading the obituaries."

The Lucky Ones

—in Canada's national newspaper

are not dead, did not die,
passed peacefully
peacefully, peacefully, peacefully,
quietly
or gently,
heedless of world news,
nestled between stocks and sports,
cherubim fluttering nearby.
Once in a while *at a time of his choosing and on her own terms*
or with uncommon specificity—*injuries resulting from a fall.*
They gust onward
—beloved, loved, loving, devoted, doting, cherished,
mourned, missed—
then double back to *love, cherish,* even *relish*
fine wine and hand-crafted salami, doodling on the family sailboat,
golf, bridge, and rescue dogs.
All the while shouldering for their kin
degrees and designations,
dissertations, innovations,
private clubs, affiliations,
and a persistent passion for planes
—six continents, ninety-five countries, many a far off land.

But best of all,
days of leisurely reading and dining al fresco
on the dock at Hornby Island or Lac Bernard.
Followed by a dip below the horizon.

Wifely Instructions

My friend Bianca was revising her will. Who to look after in the family and to what extent? What to do with her father's wartime diaries? How to endow her favourite charity—leave it the residue or make a specific gift?

As things transpired, the property part was easy. What really worried Bianca were the instructions to leave for the disposal of her body. Underground burial revolted her. Standard cremation did not meet her ecological standards. Aquamation was an option, but in her community only one funeral home offered it.

"Have you decided what you want to do with your body?" she asked me.

Well . . .

Wifely Instructions

When I'm dead
plant me in moist friable soil
teeming with the life I will resume—
protozoa, fungi, nematodes,
coyote scat, ants, Norway rats . . .
A wooden casket only if you must.
Better a bed sheet.
Please.

Let twitch grass feed on me,
and foxtail barley—
celadon feathers in spring,
supplicants blonding and bending as summer advances.
A freeway for chickarees, dusk-bandits, skunks.
Don't shave the grass to a low-pile carpet.
Please.

And can you find a place free of city noise—
back hoes and horns,
penis-driven Camaros,
flatulent Porsches,
subway trains clickety-clacking on outdoor tracks,
growling garbage trucks,
whipper snippers and lawn clippers? Oy.

A thrush?
Yes!
Or the rush of the sea.
Do you remember the hush, once upon a kirk,
on tombolo-tethered Ninian's Isle
far in the North Atlantic?

I want to rest at ease,
but I'd be lonely there.
So some place closer.
Please.

Joan's Passing

When the father of one of my colleagues died last year, the obituary, which ran in the papers for two weeks, listed the man's academic and professional credentials and traced his progression through various businesses. It detailed his social connections, association memberships, recreational past times and, of course, his family.

In the same month, a single elderly woman (whom a good friend periodically visited in a retirement residence) quietly slipped away just as he entered her room. Although I scanned the newspapers for weeks afterwards, no obituary appeared for that woman, and her funeral was a short online affair conducted by the funeral home. No spouse, children, friends, or clergy seemed to be present, and the participants could have been counted on the fingers of one hand.

Joan's Passing

A single leaf from the sycamore tree
soundless and gilt, let go and drifted down
to the leaf-littered soil that let it be.
No mite was moved, no tremor stirred the ground
the moment that it touched, no blade deposed
by such a minor nudge. It lay at ease.
And others dropped down equally composed,
their unrecorded falls a mute reprise.
They too moved not a mite nor tremor stirred
as they made contact with the ready earth
where essence is surrendered and transferred
to mystery, rid of sighs or needless words.

The tree paid scant attention though more bare,
hummed to itself, crooked elbows in the air.

Silence

George Herbert (1593–1633) served as public orator of Cambridge University before becoming an Anglican priest and a country parson. Herbert's command of language was extraordinary—he wrote in English, Latin, and Greek—but none of his poems was published during his lifetime. Herbert preferred to keep his work private but on his deathbed sent a manuscript to Nicholas Ferrar, a friend, inviting him to publish the poems only if they might be of spiritual benefit to others.

My poem "Silence" is modelled on Herbert's devotional poem, "Prayer I," a sonnet that states and restates the elusive notion of prayer.

Silence

Silence as nothingness, bottomless naught,
virginal vellum, life's pending foreword,
primaeval yolk of compressed Brahma thought,
light and eye, voice and ear and touch deferred.

Celestial song that only gods can hear,
mosses and mists emerging from the deep,
a kind of place where no one interferes,
the inward self, the mind in poetry.

Lover's knot, essence of eternity,
elided words that tell of deep rapport,
flour, water, yeast in mystic alchemy,
letters and lozenges, night table drawer.

Sky without a jet, receding freight train,
paper wasp savaging that wooden fence again.

The Transfiguration

And after six days Jesus taketh Peter, James, and John his brother, and bringeth them up into an high mountain apart, And was transfigured before them: and his face did shine as the sun, and his raiment was white as the light.

—Mathew 17:1–2 (King James Version)

The Transfiguration

Ice-air,
yew trees shuddering in concrete planters,
wind-frenzied plastic
—and Troy
back at Yonge & St. Clair
standing
tall,
walker gone.
As I pass by he takes my hand,
shakes it,
his in a bulky, black glove.
I've never touched him before.
I'm here to thank my friends for their support, he says.
I didn't know I was one of his friends.
I have a new doctor, he says,
rehab.
For the first time I notice
the perfection of his dental plate, the delicate lines plying his face.
I'm six weeks clean, he says.
Oh, I say.
Six weeks, he repeats,
as of today.
He places his right hand over his heart,
raises his chin.
It's big, he says, deep.
And suddenly he is lit, all of him is lit,
by a riveting radiance—
sun-splendour face, glowing khaki jacket,
salt-crusted boots.
Even the matted fur on his hood dazzles.

Congratulations, I say. It *is* big. And deep.
The 512 streetcar squeals past.
Wind whips up more debris.
Fuckin’ right, he says.

Index of Poems and First Lines

* Poem titles are in italic type; poem first lines are in regular type.

Earlier Publication

"After Wordsmithing" published in *Poetry Pause* by The League of Canadian Poets, March 2022

"Born to Atone" from *We Were Seeds*, published by Querencia Press, November 2024

"Botanizing with Vladimir" forthcoming in the inaugural edition of *TBR Blue*, published by *The Brussels Review*, 2025

"City Sonnet" from *The Climate Change Chronicles*, published by Bronze Bird Books, September 2024

"Encoded" from *Tiny Moments Vol IV*, published by Bronze Bird Books, July 2024

"Fall Morning Canticle" published in *Friends Journal*, October 2024

"For Halima" from *We Were Seeds*, published by Querencia Press, November 2024

"Free Radicals" from *Cities*, published by *Panorama: The Journal of Travel, Place and Nature*, July 2024

"Grandfather" from *Canada: Brave New World*, edited by Elaine Cougler, July 2023

"Highland Dithyramb" from *Summer Solstice '24*, published by Green Ink Poetry, UK

"Poets Considering Moss" published in the *Bruce Trail Conservancy Magazine*, Summer 2024

"Silence" forthcoming in the inaugural edition of *TBR Blue*, published by *The Brussels Review*, 2025

"The Joyful Wisdom" from *Death Lifespan Vol. 12*, published by Pure Slush Books Australia, July 2024

"The Orkney Hood" from *Thin Places & Sacred Spaces: An anthology of new poetry*, edited by Sarah Law, October 2024

"The Orkney Hood" published in *The Winged Moon Literary Magazine*, Hinterland, 2025

"The Raven on Summerhill" forthcoming in *POETICS: Corvids*, published by Bainbridge Island Press, 2025

"The Redress of Nature" published in *Poetry Pause* by The League of Canadian Poets, May 2023

"The Transfiguration" published in *Red Wolf Journal*, January 2025

"Unarmed Resistance" from *The Climate Change Chronicles*, published by Bronze Bird Books, September 2024

"Wifely Instructions" forthcoming in *prairiefire*, Winter 2025

"Yogurt with strains of Sogdian" published in the inaugural edition of *Al Dente*, The University of Alabama's food and place journal, December 2024

Further Reading

Has your appetite for poetry been whet, just a little? If so, you may choose to read further—nothing ponderous or impenetrable, of course—but books about poetry or the works of a particular poet who has attracted your attention. In that case, I have nine suggestions:

1. *How to Read Poetry Like a Professor,* Thomas C. Foster (2018)
   Foster's book is, hands down, my top recommendation. He takes the grandiloquence out of poetry and offers seven rules that make it accessible:

   Rule One: Read the words.
   Rule Two: Read ALL the words.
   Rule Three: Read sentences.
   Rule Four: Ignore lines on first reading.
   Rule Five: Obey all punctuation, including its absence.
   Rule Six: Read the poem aloud.
   Rule Seven: Read it again.

2. *Six Poets Hardy to Larkin,* Alan Bennett (2015)
   Bennett's book derives from his BBC series "Poetry in Motion" and confines itself to selected works by Thomas Hardy, A.E. Housman, John Betjeman, W.H. Auden, Louis MacNeice, and Phillip Larkin. I'm not deterred by his all-male choices because, as a person who reads first for primary meaning, I'm swayed by his introductory words:

   > . . . the poets and poems I chose are all in differing degrees accessible. This seemed to me essential. Obviously, any poem repays study, but if it is only to

be heard once and without detailed exposition, then a poem should be understandable at first hearing.

3. *The Making of a Poem*, Mark Strand and Eavan Boland (2000)

4. *The Discovery of Poetry*, Frances Mayes (2001)
I've paired these books, which are marginally academic, for readers attracted to poetic form. The Strand and Boland book is my go-to for clear explanations and examples of forms like the sonnet and the pantoum. The Mayes book is, as the author hoped, a field guide to the natural pleasures of language. *The natural pleasures of language*—how appealing is that?

5. *The Penguin Book of the Prose Poem*, edited by Jeremy Noel-Tod (2019)
If you are put off by the formatting of poems, the way line breaks interrupt sentences just when you're getting the hang of things, you might appreciate the prose poem, which, as the name suggests, looks more like regular text extending across a page. In this Penguin collection, Noel-Tod explains prose poetry and collects a sampling from the mid-1800s to 2017.

6. *The Norton Anthology of Poetry, Fifth Edition*, edited by Margaret Ferguson, Mary Jo Salter, and Jon Stallworthy (2005)

7. *A Book of Luminous Things*, edited by Czeslaw Milosz (1998)
Can an interested reader have too many anthologies? Possibly, so start with two:

   The Norton anthology is a classic that often shows up in free little libraries or used bookstores. I bought mine used for Can. $9.99, and it is now peppered with Post-It flags. The collection is useful if you want to know more about the work and life of poets who appeal to you. But beware: the editors assume a somewhat low level of literacy and feel obliged to point out that *lorry* means a truck, *lorries* means more than one truck, burdock is a type of weed, and "the Tempter" refers to the devil.

The Milosz anthology brings together 300 poems, both aged and contemporary, from around the world, and I commend it because Milosz had this to say about his choices:

> My proposition consists in presenting poems . . . that are, with few exceptions, short, clear, readable, and, to use a contemporary term *realist*, that is loyal toward reality and attempting to describe it as concisely as possible. Thus they undermine the widely held opinion that poetry is a misty domain eluding understanding.

8. *Into English*, edited by Martha Collins and Kevin Prufer (2017)

9. *Poems from the Edge of Extinction*, edited by Chris McCabe (2019)

Now we are into distant but meritorious waters—poems translated into English from a variety of languages. How do translators go about their work? Do they recreate a new poem from the prompts of the original? A fellow poet once posed those questions.

Into English gathers twenty-five poems written in languages such as Japanese, Turkish, and Portuguese, and presents each original followed by three different translations. The differences are fascinating. One translation may be compelling and evocative, another stilted or confusing. But which is most "true?" Without a command of the original language, you cannot say. In future, however, when you are drawn to a particular poem not originally written in English, you will know to look for alternative translations.

Poems from the Edge of Extinction takes the reader deeper into poetry and down into the tunnel of language. Editor McCabe collects poems written in endangered or vulnerable languages—Manx, Saami, Assyrian, Navaho, Rohingya, Māori, and more—and presents them in their original form, alongside an English translation and a commentary. Even if words aren't your thing, you can marvel at their range and wonder how on earth humanity came to communicate with sounds.

About the Cover Image

"That's the one!"

I was searching the internet for cover images—Kali or Artemis of Ephesus? Freyja or Quan Yin?—when Venus of Willendorf popped up, and immediately I knew she was my choice. She is neither stern nor regal nor fierce nor loving. None of the things one might look for in a god. She is . . . what?

Venus of Willendorf, a 110 millimetre limestone artefact, was familiar to me. When I led the Joseph Campbell "roundtable" in Toronto, Canada, from 2007 to 2015, we had considered her and other goddess figures from the Gravettian period (35,000–25,000 years ago). We questioned her corpulence—those haunches, thighs, breasts. Were her attributes exaggerated for effect or were they representative, perhaps of a high-status person to whom the community devoted substantial resources? One participant commented that the Venus's body resembled that of a real woman too closely to be symbolic. But, like many with theories about her, we were guessing.

The Venus of Willendorf was found on the banks of the Danube River near Willendorf, Austria, during a 1908 archeological dig. She bore traces of red paint, possibly ochre. X-ray imaging conducted more than a century later revealed fragments of bivalves in her limestone and an existing hole enlarged to form her navel.

Where did the Venus come from? Researchers sampled similar limestone from France to Ukraine and found "a strikingly close match for grain size distribution near Lake Garda in the Southern Alps (Italy)." Another close match was limestone from Isjum (Izium) in Ukraine.[14] Wherever she originated, we will never know whether the Venus was carved and carried to Willendorf or carried to Willendorf as raw material and then carved.

So many mysteries . . .

Endnotes

1 See https://www.clachtollbroch.com/ accessed 12-97-2023

2 Phrases taken from "Prayer (I)", George Herbert (1593–1633)

3 See https://www.theguardian.com/science/2016/aug/15/all-hail-the-humble-moss-bringer-of-oxygen-and-life-to-earth accessed 05-06-2023

4 See "Because of you, I burn with sorrow, God," *Rumi: Unseen Poems,* translated and edited by Brad Gooch and Maryan Mortark

5 A more detailed and authoritative explanation can be found in *Children of Ash and Elm: A History of the Vikings,* by Neil Price

6 See "Bruce Peninsula Lumber History" https://www.history-articles.com/bruce-peninsula-lumber.html accessed 05-06-2023

7 See note on page 474 of *The Complete Poems of Philip Larkin,* edited by Archie Burnett

8 Hopman, R.J., LoTemplio, S.B., Scott, E.E. et al. Resting-state posterior alpha power changes with prolonged exposure in a natural environment. Cogn. Research 5, 51 (2020). https://doi.org/10.1186/s41235-020-00247-0

9 *The Making of a Poem: A Norton Anthology of Poetic Forms*, page 8

10 https://amnesty.sa.utoronto.ca/2022/01/05/the-detention-of-the-two-michaels-a-story-on-chinas-human-rights-abuses/ 06-06-2023 "The Detention of the Two Michaels: A Story on China's Human Rights Abuses"

11 See "Younger Than War" by Mosab Abu Toha, *The Atlantic*, November 9, 2023

12 *The Masks of God: Primitive Mythology*, p. 42

13 See https://chaucer.fas.harvard.edu/pages/wife-baths-prologue-and-tale-0

14 See "The microstructure and the origin of the Venus from Willendorf" by Weber et al: https://www.nature.com/articles/s41598-022-06799-z

Gratitude and Acknowledgements

Writer and journalist Shaughnessy Bishop-Stall has a body of admirers—clients, mentees, students—and I am among them. Not only did Shaughnessy edit, order, and proofread this book, he encouraged the prose introductions. He then helped me beta-test the prose-poetry combinations. Thank you, Shaughnessy.

I also thank my beta-readers. Their initial preferences did not include poetry, but they confirmed my hunch that brief introductions, like those found in cookbooks, invite reluctant readers into poetry.

Members of the two poetry feedback groups in which I participate helped me refine and strengthen draft poems. To them, my gratitude.

Then there is my indulgent husband who tolerated random interruptions: "Hey, I need a word." "Listen to this." "How do I say . . . ?" Thank you, William.

About the Author

GENEVIEVE CHORNENKI loves working with words. For three decades she applied that love to dispute resolution, helping clients settle their differences amicably with constructive conversations, and writing educational material, including *Bypass Court: A Dispute Resolution Handbook*. But she believes words can do so much more. They can conjure places, evoke feelings, amuse people. They can be played with. What fun! Genevieve's lyrical meditation on eyesight, *Don't Lose Sight*, was published in 2021. A poet, author, editor, and literacy coach, Genevieve has had poems published in print and online in North America, Europe, and Australia. *If I Were God: Poems for People Who Don't Read Poetry* is her first collection of prose interludes and poems.

Find Genevieve online: genevievechornenki.com